Wicked Irish Wit

Aubrey Malone

summersdale

WICKED IRISH WIT

Summersdale Publishers Ltd
46 West Street
Chichester
West Sussex
PO19 1RP
UK

www.summersdale.com

Printed and bound in Great Britain

ISBN: 978-1-84024-705-3

Contents

Editor's Note

Ireland has produced some of the liveliest wordsmiths anywhere; both on the stage and on the page, and of course in the pubs, where a different type of spirit takes hold. This volume will remind you why Irish wit is known the world over, and will provide endless quips and retorts for any occasion.

Samuel Beckett once said that Irish humour consisted of five basic themes: life, death, religion, drinking and the English. This compendium brings together witty quotes and barmy one-liners on all those topics – and plenty more besides.

Verbal mischief from the likes of Oscar Wilde and Flann O'Brien through to Hal Roach and Terry Wogan is sure to leave you with a grin on your face as you delight in their gift of the gab and unpredictable profundity – as well as a generous helping of nonsense!

Laugh out loud at this veritable treasure trove, from the historical to the hysterical and the poetic to the poltroonish.

Let the craic begin…

IRISH LOGIC

An Irishman was once
asked to define winter.
'It's the time of year,'
he explained, 'when
it gets late early.'

Tom McIntyre

Large Shoes
Reduced

Sign on a shop window in Dublin

From now on it's the start
of a new beginning.

Don Givens

I'm not known outside Ireland but
I'm world famous in Dublin.

Michael Redmond

I solemnly swear that this
oath is not an oath.

Dan Breen

Happy are the parents
who have no children.

Sir Boyle Roche

In Ireland the inevitable never
happens and the unexpected
constantly occurs.

John Pentland Mahaffy

I wouldn't mind the rain if
it wasn't for the wet.

Jim Shanahan

If my father was alive to see the
modern world, he'd turn in his grave.

Michael O'Doherty

❧

The only way of preventing
what is past is to put a stop
to it before it happens.

Sir Boyle Roche

❧

Rainbows aren't optical illusions.
They only look like them.

Jimeoin

Closed on Account of Re-opening

Sign on a shop window, Cork

If it wasn't for half the people
in the world, the other half
would be all of them.

Michael Redmond

The first two-syllable word
I learned when I was growing
up was 'discretion'.

Eamon Dunphy

When Corkonians mean
'Never', they say, 'I will, yeah.'

David Monaghan

———◆———

My father discovered a cure for
amnesia but forgot what it was.

Noel Purcell

———◆———

The only thing that has to
be finished by next Friday
is next Thursday.

Maureen Potter

When I was young I used to think I
was indecisive but now I'm not so sure.

Eoin Carey

When I believe in the discipline of silence so
much I could talk for hours about it.

George Bernard Shaw

Women, Without Distinction
of Sex, Will Be Served.

Notice on Irish pub window

The Irish love to be loved,
except by each other.

David Kenny

THE GOLDEN YEARS

We're not the men
our fathers were. If
we were we would
be terribly old.

Flann O'Brien

I do, and I hope to
have it replaced
very soon.

Terry Wogan on people saying he
didn't know the meaning of 'hip'

You know you're growing
old when the light of your life
is the one in the fridge.

Hal Roach

———◆———

No woman should ever be
quite accurate about her age.
It looks so calculating.

Oscar Wilde

———◆———

They say you're only as old
as you feel. In which case I
probably died six years ago.

Joe O'Connor

I don't do drugs. If I want a rush I just stand up when I'm not expecting to.

Dylan Moran

Granny said she was going to grow old gracefully, but she left it too late.

Christine Kelly

As long as a woman
can look ten years
younger than her
daughter, she is
perfectly satisfied.

Oscar Wilde

PINT-SIZED WISDOM

Only in Ireland is
the pint of stout
regarded as a digestif.

Terry Wogan

I have too much blood
in my alcohol stream.

Richard Harris

In England I'm regarded as
an alcoholic. In Ireland they
see me as a sissy drinker.

Shane MacGowan

—◆—

Ring Irish Alcoholics. If you
fancy sobering up, someone
comes round with a Guinness.

Seamus O'Leary

—◆—

Irish whisky makes you see
double and feel single.

Peter Cagney

I once knew a guy who thought
'loading the dishwasher' meant
getting his wife drunk.

Sil Fox

⚬—•—⚬

Goliath couldn't handle his
liquor. David gave him one
shot and he got stoned.

Ardal O'Hanlon

⚬—•—⚬

Ireland is the only country in the
world where there are protestors
outside AA meetings.

Des Bishop

I slept like a baby. Every three hours
I woke up looking for a bottle.

Liam O'Reilly

⬥

I hardly ever suffered from morning
sickness when I was pregnant
because I was so used to hangovers.

Caitlin Thomas

⬥

The question of whether the glass
is half full or half empty depends on
whether you're drinking or pouring.

Richard Harris

My mother used to say it was all
right to drink with a nun as long
as you didn't get into the habit.

Vincent Dowling

❧

The reason I went to America
was because I saw a sign saying
'Drink Canada Dry'.

George Best

❧

I drink therefore I am. I'm
drunk therefore I was.

Seamus O'Leary

IN FOR A PENNY

If anyone broke into
our house, they'd
leave a donation.

Frank Carson

I'm not a bourgeois decadent
yet, but I'm saving up for it.

Brendan Behan

❦

It is better to have a permanent
income than to be fascinating.

Oscar Wilde

❦

You say stupid things to
people you're in love with.
Like: 'Here's all my money'.

Sean Hughes

Our father used to sit us on the po and tell us ghost stories.

Big O talking about his father's
alternatives to laxatives

Nothing is more expensive than a
girl who's free for the evening.

Hal Roach

Tea is the champagne of the poor.

Hugh Leonard

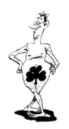

LIGHTS, CAMERA, ACTION

That's the closest
to a knighthood
I'll ever get.

Daniel Day-Lewis after being presented
with an Oscar by Helen 'The Queen'
Mirren at the 2008 Oscar ceremony

I've played so many priests in films, when we sit down to eat, our entire family discusses everything in Latin.

Pat O'Brien

Hollywood buys a good story about a bad girl and changes it to a bad story about a good girl.

Richard Harris

Colin Farrell is more
Irish in Hollywood
than he ever was at
home in Dublin.

Jane Kelly

BATTLE OF THE SEXES

The weaker sex is
actually the stronger
sex – because of
the weakness of
the stronger sex for
the weaker sex.

Frank Hall

Life is one fool thing after
another, whereas love is two
fool things after each other.

Oscar Wilde

Don't let a kiss fool you
or a fool kiss you.

Frankie Byrne

For a young girl to be named
'wholesome' is perhaps the
deadliest insult of all.

Caitlin Thomas

Dates are only
for the police.

Brendan Behan

A nice girl is one who whispers
sweet nothing-doings into your ear.

James Healy

❦

I think, therefore I'm single.

Sinead Flynn

❦

I like men who have a future
and women who have a past.

Oscar Wilde

Changeable women are more endurable than monotonous ones. They are sometimes murdered, but rarely deserted.

George Bernard Shaw

HEAVENLY PURSUITS

Irish atheists have started a 'Dial-A-Prayer' service. When they phone, nobody answers.

Hal Roach

Do you have to believe
in God to be a nun?

Rosie O'Donnell

———◆———

The reason God created Adam
before he created Eve was
because he didn't want anyone
telling him how to create Adam.

Stephen Maguire

———◆———

All the things we loathe
in human beings are the
attributes we give to God.

David Feherty

God's only excuse is that
he doesn't exist.

Samuel Beckett

———

Opportunity only knocks once.
If there's a second one, it's
probably a Jehovah's Witness.

John O'Connor

———

I believe everything the Catholic
Church teaches is true, but I let
my wife go to Mass for me.

Brendan Behan

I'd love to shoot the Pope
– because I know he'd forgive me.

Tommy Tiernan

I once played God in a play and
my wife said it was typecasting.

Vincent Dowling

I used to look on God as a kind
of celestial Jeremy Beadle.

Marian Keyes

On his passport
where it says
'Place of Birth', he
wrote 'Manger'.

Ed O'Halloran talking about Bono

It is sad. One half of the world does not believe in God, and the other half does not believe in me.

Oscar Wilde

———•———

Extremist Catholics and extremist Protestants should get together to get rid of ecumenism.

Liam Desmond

———•———

Why is it that people you wish had never been born are always the ones who get born again?

Joe O'Connor

Why do we never hear about
lapsed Protestants?

Dave Allen

❧

If the Virgin Mary was assumed
bodily into heaven, where
does she go to the toilet?

Anne Enright

❧

Every saint has a past, and
every sinner a future.

Callum Best

I'm a bad Catholic. It's the
religion of all great artists.

Brendan Behan

How much can I get away with
and still go to heaven?

Quentin Roundtree

Ireland remains a deeply divided
country, the two main denominations
being 'us' and 'them'.

Frank McNally

When the gods wish to punish
us they answer our prayers.

Oscar Wilde

Wanted: Man and woman to look
after two cows, both Protestant.

Ad in Belfast newspaper

Would a born-again Christian
have two belly buttons?

Noel V. Ginnity

St Patrick brought Christianity
to Ireland. It's a pity the
idea never caught on.

George Bernard Shaw

How I wish that Adam had died
with all his bones in his body!

Dion Boucicault

There's no such thing
as original sin. Just
use your imagination
on some existing ones.

Sil Fox

FUNNY PHRASES

One swallow doesn't
make a pint.

Richard Harris

True friends stab you in the front.

Oscar Wilde

—◆—

If you touch an electric
fence on purpose, does it
still count as a shock?

Mark Doherty

Obviously crime
pays. What criminal
would be stupid
enough to go to
prison for nothing?

Gerard Gormley

Nothing succeeds like excess.

Oscar Wilde

———

Happiness can't buy money.

Maureen Potter

———

Love may make the world go round, but not as fast as whisky.

Richard Harris

If you stop and
smell the roses,
sooner or later
you'll inhale a bee.

Seamus Thornton

LITERARY LIVES

I write like a snail
trailing slime. But
sometimes the
slime glistens.

John Banville

Wilfred Owen is all about blood,
dirt and a sucked sugar stick.

W. B. Yeats

—◆◦◆—

Writing poems is like mining.
One day you get some silver,
and the next you just get rock.

Eavan Boland

—◆◦◆—

The first rule for a young playwright
to follow is not to write like Henry
Arthur Jones. The second
and third rules are the same.

Oscar Wilde

Never judge a book by its movie.

Cyril Cusack

❧

The most famous Irish short story,
'The Dead', is famous for, among
other things, not being very short.

Frank McNally

❧

I once wrote a book on
humility. I think it's my best.

Michael Crawley

Libel letters are the
Oscars of journalism.

Roisin Ingle

———❖———

If you asked Yeats for bread he
didn't exactly give you a stone. He
gave you a finely polished pebble.

Monk Gibbon

———❖———

James Joyce was a true artist
from his head to his crotch.

Alec Guinness

If an Irishman says
he's a writer, give
him a sobriety test.
If he flunks it he's
telling the truth.

Henry Spalding

Today's newspaper is
tomorrow's toilet paper.

Barry Fitzgerald

———————

The only really dirty four-
lettered word is 'work'.

Brendan Kennelly

———————

Most poets who offer you advice
should be ignored because
they want you to be just like
them, only not quite so good.

Adrian Mitchell

Only a new cure for the clap could possibly justify all the circumambient peripherisation of *Finnegans Wake*.

Ezra Pound

Anybody can write a three-volume novel. It merely requires a complete ignorance of both life and literature.

Oscar Wilde

Sometimes I read a book with pleasure and detest the author.

Jonathan Swift

There's no tribe of human
beings more pestiferous than
the people who insist on lending
you books whether you wish
to borrow them or not.

Robert Lynd

Jonathan Swift is an occasional
poet who sings lightly about
dandruff, drains, body odour, dirty
underclothes and comic farts.

Tom Paulin

Good readers are almost
as rare as good writers.

John Banville

Good stories write themselves.
Bad ones have to be written.

F. Scott Fitzgerald

Ulysses was popular in the United
States because Americans
love crossword puzzles.

Oliver St John Gogarty

I loved the idea of doing law, but
I hated reading books, which
could have been a problem.

Bryan McFadden

A poet can survive anything
but a misprint.

Oscar Wilde

My dear sir, I have read your
play. Oh my dear, sir!

Rejection notice from F. Scott Fitzgerald

Murder is considered less immoral
than fornication in literature.

George Moore

Like all good drama critics, we
retired to the pub across the road.

Eric Cross

———— • ————

What is Joseph Conrad but
the wreck of Robert Louis
Stevenson floating about on
the slip-slop of Henry James?

George Moore

———— • ————

Come forth, Lazarus! And he
came fifth and lost his job.

James Joyce, *Ulysses*

Jonathan Swift
was something of a
rarity among famous
Irish writers in that
he actually lived and
wrote in Ireland.

Evan McHugh

BE A SPORT

I've seen big men
hide in corridors
to avoid him.

Martin O'Neill on Brian Clough

Since Italia 1990, every
Irishman learned four words
of Italian, 'Olé, olé, olé, olé.'
Except they were Spanish.

Niall Tobin

Maradona was the highest-
paid handballer in history.

Con Houlihan

Ray Treacy got 56 caps for Ireland,
and 30 of those were for his singing.

Eamon Dunphy

Alex Higgins isn't looking too
well recently. He's obviously
not getting enough greens.

Dennis Taylor

❧

You always know where Frank
Carson is on a golf course
because you can hear him
– unless he's doing well.

Tom O'Connor

❧

People slag me off about
my right foot, but without it
I couldn't use my left.

John Morley

A newspaper headline you'll
never get to see: 'Police Warn of
Trouble From Golf Hooligans.'

Robert O'Byrne

❦

Ollie Murphy throws more
dummies than a baby in a crèche.

Kevin Mallon

❦

Peter Clohessy's main
problem was that he couldn't
stop jumping on hookers.

Dermot Morgan

Of course I have played outdoor
games. I once played dominoes
in an open-air cafe in Paris.

Oscar Wilde

Old golfers don't die.
They just putter out.

Sil Fox

No comment – and don't
quote me on that.

Mick McCarthy

Norman Whiteside was more
a scorer of great goals rather
than a great scorer of goals.

Paul McGrath

Show me a dressing room of nice
polite players and I'll show you
a dressing room full of losers.

Tony Cascarino

In the first half they played with
the wind. In the second half
they played with the ball.

Mícheál Ó Muircheartaigh

Chelsea has just launched a new aftershave called 'The Special One' by U Go Boss.

Pat Flanagan on José Mourinho's departure in 2007

A golf club is a stick with a head on one end and a fool at the other.

Damien Muldoon

I gave up shadow-boxing the night my shadow beat me up.

James McKeon

The first half was even, but
the second was even worse.

Pat Spillane

He didn't get booked
for the yellow card.

Frank Stapleton

I wasn't long in training before
I tore a stomach muscle, which
was a real pain in the ass.

Mick McCarthy

His strength, or strengths,
are his strength.

Boxing commentator Mick Dowling

—◆—

A farmer could make a tidy
living in the amount of ground it
takes Moss Keane to turn.

Danny Lynch

—◆—

That performance would
have won him Olympic gold in
the championship four years
ago, which he won anyway.

Des Lynam

Mark Brooks could finish his swing under a coffee table.

David Feherty

Keep your high balls
low into the wind.

John B. Keane repeating advice given
to him as a young footballer

There are those who believe
an intelligent Kerry footballer
is one whose IQ is higher
than his shirt number.

Pat Spillane

The rules of Meath football
are simple. If it moves, kick it. If
it doesn't, kick it until it does.

Martin Gorman

The last time we played in
Seville we got beat two-nil.
And we were lucky to get nil.

Mick McCarthy

❧

I'm suffering from repetitive
strain injury. It comes from
going 'Putt, putt, putt.'

Val Doonican

❧

Doctors who golf have one
advantage over the rest: nobody
can read their scorecards.

Noel V. Ginnity

I used to be as good at drinking
as Tiger Woods is at golf.

David Feherty

Paul McGrath's knees are gone
again. It's terrible what a bottle
of vodka can do to a body.

Bobby Devlin

WORLDLY WISE

For many years I
though an innuendo
was an Italian
suppository.

Spike Milligan

A Mexican straight
flush is any five
cards and a gun.

Hugh Leonard

De Valera is the greatest
Irishman born in New York to a
Spanish father who ever lived.

Pat Fitzpatrick

One always loves the country
one has conquered, and I
have conquered England.

George Bernard Shaw

The next nuclear war will be
held in London so England
won't have to qualify.

Dermot Morgan

The Irish remember too much
and the English too little.

Eilis O'Hanlon

———•———

Being an Englishwoman, she held
the curious theory that the police
exist for the protection of the public.

George Birmingham

———•———

Americans will go on adoring me until
I say something nice about them.

George Bernard Shaw

The English character is fearful of
intellectuals in a way that Dracula
had a thing about crosses.

Declan Lynch

The British beatitudes are
beer, business, bibles, bulldogs,
battleships, buggery and bishops.

James Joyce

Britain might once have
ruled the waves. But now it's
reduced to waiving the rules.

Gerry Adams

I don't like German. It isn't at all a becoming language. I know perfectly well that I look quite plain after my German lesson.

Oscar Wilde

HOME TRUTHS

An Irishman was
asked if the Irish
always answered
one question with
another. 'Who told
you that?' he replied.

Niall Toibin

One of the good things about
modern Ireland is that you
don't have to hang around in
libraries any more to get warm.

Roddy Doyle

Ireland is America's 52nd state.

Noel Browne

The Irish, and I'm also guilty of this,
think they invented everything.

Bono

Being an aristocrat in Ireland is a
bit of a millstone, but it does get
you a good seat in a restaurant.

Lord Inchiquin

I finally found a diet that
works in Ireland. I only eat
when the weather's good.

Hal Roach

Capital punishment means
having to live in Dublin.

Sean Kilroy

Dublin University contains the cream of Ireland – rich and thick.

Samuel Beckett

—•—

Irish racing is like 'Fiddler on the Hoof'.

Brendan McGahon.

—•—

I was born Irish and have continued to be so all my life.

Colonel Saunderson

In Ireland most complaints
are made with a whisper.

David Monaghan

If you succeed in Ireland it's
like, 'Who do you think you are?
I knew you were nothing.'

Bob Geldof

A secret in Dublin means just
telling one person at a time.

Ciarán MacGonigal

If you don't drink or snort coke
or sleep with Colin Farrell,
there's nothing to do in Dublin.

Sinéad O'Connor

The term 'Irish Secret Service'
is as big a contradiction as
'British Intelligence'.

David Norris

Being a woman is like being
Irish. Everyone says you're
important and nice, but you
always take second place.

Iris Murdoch

Did you hear about
the Kerryman with the
inferiority complex?
He thought he was
only as good as
everyone else.

John B. Keane

TROUBLE AND STRIFE

I'm hoarse listening to
my wife complaining.

Brendan Behan

A man will kill his wife and then kill himself. A woman kills her husband, then does her nails.

Thomas Lynch

Marriage is forever – like cement.

Peter O'Toole

❧

We had a quiet wedding. Her father had a silencer on the shotgun.

Sean Kilroy

❧

If there were no husbands, who would look after our mistresses?

George Moore

I'm married to a very dear
girl who's an artist. We have
no children except me.

Brendan Behan

How marriage ruins a man. It's
as demoralising as cigarettes,
and far more expensive.

Oscar Wilde

I don't tell my wife anything. I
figure that what she doesn't
know won't hurt me.

Danny Cummins

A man who says his wife can't take
a joke forgets that she took him.

Oscar Wilde

———————

A mother-in-law dies when
another devil is needed in hell.

Sean Kilroy

———————

I'm giving up marriage for Lent.

Brian Behan

God sent the Irish to
Canada to keep them from
marrying Protestants.

Mavis Gallant

Give women the vote and in
five years' time there will be a
crushing tax on bachelors.

George Bernard Shaw

The ideal wife for an Irishman is a
rich dumb blonde nymphomaniac
who owns a pub near a racecourse.

Sean Kilroy

Never make a task a pleasure,
as the man said when he dug his
wife's grave only three feet deep.

Seamus McManus

The only thing my husband
ever achieved on his own
was his moustache.

Jane O'Reilly

A dead wife under the table is the
best goods in a man's house.

Jonathan Swift

Clodagh and Pat
have just ended a
life-long friendship.
They got married.

Peter Cagney

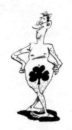

LET'S FACE THE MUSIC

The can-can from *Orpheus in the Underworld* isn't great for dancing unless you can-can, and I can't.

Vincent Dowling

George Bernard Shaw has
the emotional range of a Pat
Boone record with a scratch.

A. A. Gill

Ronan Keating wants to be
Robbie Williams, but what he
really is is Cliff Richard.

Louis Walsh

I'm old enough to remember Elvis
the first time he was alive.

Noel V. Ginnity

I have no regrets other than an
awful haircut in the mid-eighties
which launched a thousand
third division soccer players.

Bono

If there's music in hell,
it'll be bagpipes.

Joe Tomelty

I just saw 'Sold Out' on a
placard outside a Bob Dylan
concert. Wasn't that in 1966
when he went electric?

Hugh Kenny

Though I can see Jim Morrison's
star appeal, I could write better
poetry than that pissed.

Fran Cosgrave

I should have realised Mark
Feehilly was gay when he told
me he liked Mariah Carey.

Louis Walsh

If Chris Rea joined
up with Dire Straits,
they could call
themselves Diarrhoea.

Eanna Brophy

The songs Johnny Cash
produced with Rick Rubin
probably extended his life. But
they probably shortened mine.

Damien Fitzpatrick

Boy George can't make up his
mind whether he wants to work with
Robbie Williams or beat him up.

Ian O'Doherty

If I have nothing to say, that's
the first line of the song.

Bono

People forget that when
Elvis was alive, you couldn't
give his records away.

Michael O'Riordan

Pretty woman my arse.

Bono's father after meeting Julia Roberts

If a woman's genitalia could
sing, it'd sound like Enya.

Dylan Moran

Madonna's figure looks fantastic
considering it's only eight weeks
since she bought a baby.

Graham Norton

The bloody crowd were so dry
tonight, they were farting dust.

Liam Ivory

I'm looking for compensation for
psychological stress caused by
the Barbara Streisand concert.
I could hear her singing.

Shane Horgan

His vibrato sounded like he was driving a tractor over ploughed fields with weights tied to his scrotum.

Spike Milligan

The bagpipes were given to the Scots by the Irish, but the Scots haven't seen the joke yet.

Tom O'Connor

Simon Cowell's waxwork in Madame Tussauds is more real than he is.

Louis Walsh

YOU ARE WHAT
YOU EAT

Fast food is
something you eat
during Lent.

Tom McDevitt

Cooking isn't my girlfriend's forte.
She uses a smoke alarm as a timer.

Paddy Dolan

The second day of a diet is always
easier than the first, because by
the second day you're off it.

Dusty Young

I once went on a three-week
diet... and lost 21 days.

Jack Leonard

Why do people who only drink tea say to their friends, 'Let's meet for coffee'?

Jackie Fitzgerald

A hot dog feeds the
hand that bites it.

Derek Davis

❦

I know I'm putting on weight. It
usually coincides with me breathing.

Marian Keyes

❦

The journey of a thousand pounds
begins with a single burger.

Chris O'Brien

She swears she diets
religiously. She doesn't eat
while she's in church.

Hal Roach

❦

Thirteen out of every ten women
prefer chocolate to maths.

Steven Scally

❦

After a good dinner one can forgive
anybody, even one's own relations.

Oscar Wilde

I didn't fight my way to the top of
the food chain to be a vegetarian.

Joe O'Herlihy

———◆———

I have just given up spinach for Lent

F. Scott Fitzgerald

———◆———

A restaurant I used to frequent in
Cork advertised: 'Eat here and
you'll never eat anywhere else again.'

Niall Toibin

I'm a light eater. As soon as
it's light, I start eating.

Brendan Grace

———◆———

Her heart is in the right place. It's
a pity the other 15 stone isn't.

Frank Carson

———◆———

Someone said to me the other
day, 'Shall we eat or will we
have a McDonald's?'

Dave Allen

ADVICE AND CONSENT

Love your enemies
– just in case your
friends turn out to be
a bunch of bastards.

R. A. Dickson

Never speak when you're angry.
If you do, you'll make the best
speech you'll ever regret.

Robert Lynd

Do not love your neighbour as
yourself. If you are on good terms
with yourself it is impertinence.

George Bernard Shaw

Never hit an Irishman when he's
down. He might get up again.

Seamus O'Leary

Only one part of
the body must not
move during an Irish
dance – the bowels.

Jack McHale

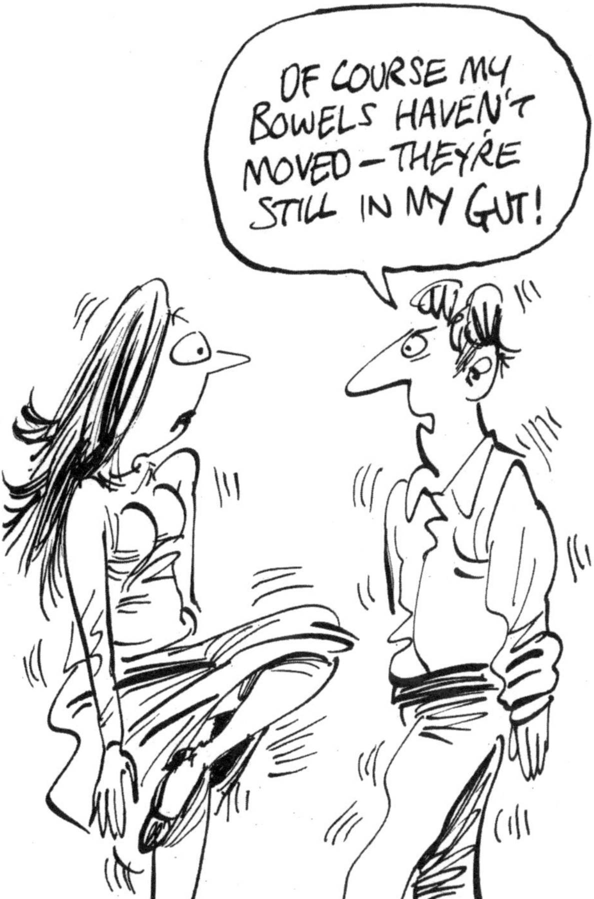
OF COURSE MY BOWELS HAVEN'T MOVED – THEY'RE STILL IN MY GUT!

How do you cross Dublin without passing a pub? Go into all of them!

James Joyce

———•———

Never hit a man with glasses. Use a brick.

Seamus O'Leary

———•———

In any controversy it's the safest to assume both sides are lying.

Robert Lynd

If you want to do a deal in
Hollywood, first join the
Beverly Hills AA.

Mary Kenny

Don't go to bed mad. Stay
up and plot your revenge.

Paul Casey

Many hands make light work,
so put them all up to the bulb
in the event of power failure.

Michael Sheridan

Never eat on an empty stomach.

Jason Byrne

—◆—

Drink is your enemy.
Love your enemies.

Sil Fox

—◆—

The best cure for a hangover
is hangover sex.

Declan Lynch

Keep Ireland beautiful.
Shoot your mother-in-law.

Sean Kilroy

Abstinence should always be
practised in moderation.

Joe Lynch

Always buy a good bed and
a good pair of shoes. You're
usually in one or the other.

Gloria Hunniford

My advice to stand-up comedians? Wear a pair of brown trousers.

Danny La Rue

READY TO WEAR

No, that skirt doesn't
make you look fatter.
How could it?

Maureen Potter

The law is like a
woman's knickers
– full of dynamite
and elastic.

John B. Keane

A really well-made buttonhole is the only link between Art and Nature.

Oscar Wilde

I'm a drag addict, not a drug addict.

Boy George

If a man buys his girlfriend a see-through dress, his motives are transparent.

Sinéad Cusack

The main thing man enjoys about a woman's clothes are his fantasies about how she'd look without them.

Brendan Francis

When we went to a party, Dylan would often leave with a better coat than when he arrived.

Caitlin Thomas

My wife isn't so smart. She has to reach into her bra to count to two.

Tommy Dempsey

A transistor is a nun who
wears men's clothes.

Sean Kilroy

The latest thing in men's
clothes is women.

Paul O'Grady

Men's main exercise at the beach
consists of sucking in their stomachs
every time they see a girl in a bikini.

Geoff Fennell

I'm all into self-improvement. I turn my underwear inside out once a week.

Richard Crowley

Women are wearing dresses so short these days they'll soon have four cheeks to powder.

Dave Allen

Statistics are like bikinis. What they reveal is interesting; what they don't reveal is even more so.

Chris Barry

Most chick lit could be subtitled
'The Joy of Clothes'.

Ann-Marie Hourihane

There's probably something good
that can be said about corsets,
but I just can't think of what it is.

Maureen Potter

Irish brothers, it's truly time that we
changed. Our habits. Our thinking.
Our socks once a fortnight.

Joe O'Connor

If you dress the part
in golf, people believe
you can actually play.

Eamonn Holmes

SEXPOTS

I bought a four-poster bed once and started making little notches. It collapsed after a week.

George Best

A eunuch is a man cut
out to be a bachelor.

Sean Kilroy

Sex is one game never postponed
because of darkness.

Sean Kilroy

A pretty girl said to a pensioner,
'Let's go upstairs and make love'.
He replied, 'I can't do both.'

Big O

I've always thought
of sex as a bit like
blowing your nose.

Maeve Binchy

Academy awards are like orgasms.
Only a few of us know the
feeling of having multiple ones.

John Huston

—◆—

Safe sex to a Dubliner is doing it
when your wife's gone to bingo.

David Kenny

—◆—

The town I come from was
so conservative, the local
hooker was a virgin.

Tom Murtagh

We've got the pigs out of the
parlour but we haven't yet shifted
the bishops out of the bedroom.

James Downey

—◆—

They say I slept with seven
Miss Worlds. That's untrue.
It was only four. I didn't turn
up for the other three.

George Best

—◆—

Chastity is curable if
detected early enough.

Cyril Cusack

The three best things in
life are a drink before and
a cigarette afterwards.

Seamus O'Leary

I'll tell you what separates the men
from the boys: the sodomy laws.

George Carlin

Having sex while drunk is like
trying to squeeze a marshmallow
into a piggybank.

Tommy Tiernan

The Catholic Church offers
women the choice of perpetual
virginity or perpetual pregnancy.

Dave Allen

I once made a pass at a bisexual
but was rejected on both counts.

Michael Maher

Is adultery a sin only
adults can commit?

John Banville

I've written every possible kind
of sex scene except a couple
doing it standing in a hammock.

Lee Dunne

———◆———

A psychiatrist is a sex maniac
who failed the practicals.

Sean Kilroy

———◆———

Irish maternity hospitals have
a ten-month waiting list.

Seamus O'Leary

Catholics believe you
can't have sex unless
you're a) married
or b) a bishop.

Patrick Kielty

MEA CULPA

My idea of exercise
is striking a match
for a cigarette.

Anne-Marie Scanlon

If suffering brings wisdom, I
would wish to be less wise.

W. B. Yeats

I don't like knowing what people
say behind my back. It makes
me far too conceited.

Oscar Wilde

My singing voice is like an aural fart.

Graham Norton

I'm not a philosopher. Guilty bystander, that's my role.

Peter O'Toole

———— ·•· ————

I had a rough childhood. I was breastfed by my father.

James McKeon

———— ·•· ————

Television is full of people like me – inverted egomaniacs.

Terry Wogan

My father had a profound influence on me. He was a lunatic.

Spike Milligan

———•———

There are days when I make Joan Crawford look like Mother Teresa.

Boy George

———•———

When I'm playing football, there's nothing I enjoy as much as making a fool out of some other player.

George Best

My religion? Orthodox coward.

Brendan Behan

———◆———

I'm a paranoid in reverse. I suspect people of plotting to make me happy.

Dave Allen

———◆———

I'm a geriatric novelty with a brogue.

Frank McCourt

I was a slow developer.
I didn't develop my first
birthmark until I was five.

James McKeon

I'm not so sure if I believe in
reincarnation. I can't even remember
the things I've done in this life.

Richard Harris

I have so little regard for
myself I didn't even invite
myself to my own wedding.

Colin Farrell

If people had been able to read my thoughts I'd have been locked up years ago.

Anne-Marie Scanlon

—◆—

I looked like a baked bean until I was 13.

Bono

—◆—

I can resist everything except temptation.

Oscar Wilde

I'm Irish. We think sideways.

Spike Milligan

I always start writing with a clean
piece of paper and a dirty mind.

Patrick Dennis

I always know it when women
don't like me. They say things
like, 'Yeah, that's him officer.'

Kevin Brennan

The only thing I ever passed
at school was worms.

James McKeon

———•———

I lost so many years through drink,
it was 1972 before I learned
JFK had been assassinated.

David Kelly

———•———

I'm a dancer trapped inside
the body of a tree.

Ardal O'Hanlon

All I want to do is
sit on my arse, fart
and think of Dante.

Samuel Beckett

TWO-FINGERED
SALUTES

Alex Higgins once
called me a 13 ½
stone bag of shit.

Dennis Taylor

Because they were extinguished
looking as opposed to
distinguished looking, I divined
that they were journalists.

Con Houlihan

❖

A critic is a person who will
slit the throat of a skylark to
see what makes it sing.

J. M. Synge

❖

In the human race, you came last.

Spike Milligan

He'd be out of
his depth on a
wet pavement.

Joe O'Shea

She has an ego like a raging tooth.

W. B. Yeats

I can't stand media people
interviewing each other. It reminds
me of ingrown toenails.

Brendan O'Regan

If you had a brain cell, it
would die of loneliness.

John O'Dwyer

If I say that he's extremely
stupid, I don't mean that in
any derogatory sense.

Brendan O'Carroll

❧

Your features don't seem to
know the value of teamwork.

Gene Fitzpatrick

❧

My wife is the kind of woman who
gives necrophilia a bad name.

Patrick Murray

She had all the characteristics
of a poker, with the exception
of its occasional warmth.

Daniel O'Donnell

———◆———

Donncha O'Dulaing has his place.
It's a small jail in Guatemala.

Dermot Morgan

———◆———

My father is so long on the
dole he thinks a P45 is a gun.

Big O

176

Colin Farrell's TV interviews
have more beeps than the
M50 at rush hour.

Anita Mullan

❦

The inner city architecture of
Dublin is like a lady in the morning
without her make-up on.

Jim Tunney

❦

Jonathan Swift hated his
neighbour as much as himself.

W. B. Yeats

I loved her so much
I named my first
ulcer after her.

Dusty Young

CORRIDORS OF POWER

The weak are a long
time in politics.

Barry Egan

An Irish politician's smile is like
moonlight on a tombstone.

Sean Kilroy

❧

I don't like political jokes. Too
many of them get elected.

Donal Foley

❧

In the United States anybody
can become president.
That's the problem.

George Carlin

Ireland has the best politicians
money can buy.

Sam Snort

My electioneering style? I
kiss the mothers and shake
hands with the babies.

Joe Costello

Don't vote. The government
always gets in.

Frank Kelly

Why do you stand for
election to get a seat?

Donal Foley

————◆————

A man should always be drunk
when he talks of politics. It's the
only way to make them important.

Seán O'Casey

————◆————

Haughey and his entourage
were a collection of over-
dressed bookies' runners.

Brendan O' Heithir

182

The Greeks came up with
democracy, but they had no
intention of everyone having it.

Bono

❦

The only place where success comes
before work is in a dictionary.

Sean Lemass

❦

If enough women march out
of step together, suddenly
you've got an army.

Marian Keyes

A once-fine champion of the
underdog, Ireland's Labour
Party now has all the weight
of an anorexic tadpole.

David Kelly

The main qualification for being
a royal is to smile constantly
and pretend you're having a
great time everywhere.

Maeve Binchy

I was once thrown out of
the Anarchist Party.

Brendan Behan

If John Major was drowning,
his whole life would pass before
him... and he wouldn't be in it.

Dave Allen

The toilets at Buckingham Palace
were lovely. It's nice to feel you've
been able to leave something behind.

Gloria Hunniford

If Bertie Ahern is a socialist,
then the moon is a balloon and
Tony Blair never told a lie.

Eamonn McCann

My father said Dev was so crooked, if he swallowed a six-inch nail, he'd shit a corkscrew.

Fergal Keane

If Irish politicians were laid end-to-end, they'd have their feet in each other's mouths.

Seamus O'Leary

Arnold Schwarzenegger is the governor of California. He got there by lifting things.

Dylan Moran

SCATTERED THOUGHTS

I would like to divide
my life into alternative
periods of penance,
cavorting and work.

Edna O'Brien

The less you do, the less
mistakes you make.

Bernie Comaskey

❧

Anger with stupidity is the
most exhausting of emotions.

W. B. Yeats

❧

A lot of warm vulgarity is
incomparably preferable to a
little bit of pinched niceness.

Caitlin Thomas

The day after tomorrow is the
third day of the rest of your life.

George Carlin

I understand life isn't fair,
but why couldn't it just once
be unfair in my favour?

Christy Murphy

The betting man is enviable for
only one thing: he knows what
to talk about to barbers.

Robert Lynd

It's not how you deal with
success that defines you, but
how you deal with failure.

Claire Byrne

———◆———

Life is much too important a thing
ever to talk seriously about it.

Oscar Wilde

THE ANIMAL KINGDOM

It was so hot out today, I saw a Dalmatian with his spots on the ground.

Pat McCormick

While vacationing in Africa I got
to swim with the sharks – which
didn't scare me after Riverdance.

Michael Flatley

In Bandon, even the pigs
are Protestant.

David Monaghan

The last time a mosquito bit
me, it had to sign into the Betty
Ford Clinic for detox.

Richard Harris

Do chickens get people pox?

Maureen Potter

Did you hear about the dog
who went to the flea circus?
He stole the show.

Jack Cruise

My dog's been eating
garlic. His bark's
worse than his bite.

Paul Malone

It's the neighbour's cat that makes
one believe there is a hell.

Robert Lynd

You don't need a licence for a
cat. Mankind wouldn't dare.

Pat Ingoldsby

Tarzan's yell was made up from a
blend of a camel's bleat, hyena's
yowl and a plucked violin.

Maureen O'Sullivan

Why do we wait until a pig is dead before we cure it?

Danny Cummins

A cat is a crossword puzzle with no clues.

Mac O' Brien

My dog is half Labrador, half pit bull. She bites my leg off and then brings it back to me.

Frank Carson

Cats are the fascists of
the animal world.

Brendan Behan

———— ·•· ————

All the animals went into
Noah's Ark in pairs, but the
worms went in apples.

James McKeon

———— ·•· ————

If one person calls you a
donkey, ignore him. If two
people do it, buy a saddle.

Austin O'Malley

Every dog has its
day, but only a dog
with a broken tail
has a weak end.

Seamus O'Leary

THE BIG SLEEP

I watched a funeral go by and asked who was dead. A man said, 'The fella in the box.'

Dave Allen

There's no point taking out life insurance. My uncle did and he died all the same.

Sean Kilroy

I like Italian graves. They look so much more lived in.

Elizabeth Bowen

He was at death's door, but the doctor pulled him through.

Frank Carson

I find if I don't die in autumn I always
seem to survive until Christmas.

Richard Brinsley Sheridan

I woke up this morning and I'm
still alive, so I'm pretty cheerful.

Spike Milligan

I intend to die in bed at 110
writing poetry, sipping Guinness
and serenading a woman.

Richard Harris

I'd prefer to be dead than
allow myself to be buried in
a Protestant graveyard.

Brendan Grace

—•—

I was disturbed by not being
disturbed at my father's death.

Vincent Dowling

—•—

An undertaker is the last
man to let you down.

Jimmy O'Dea

An optimist is someone on Death Row who's also a member of Weight Watchers.

Kevin Flynn

Life is overrated. Two-thirds of
it is a 'lie' and half of it is 'if'.

Denis Buckley

When I die I want fine fat-arsed
horses to take me to the cemetery,
not skinny old knackers.

Christine English

Men talk of killing time, while
time quietly kills them.

Dion Boucicault

Funerals should be called funferalls.

James Joyce

You die of a heart attack with
the Atkins diet, but so what?
At least you die thin.

Bob Geldof

www.summersdale.com